■ SCHOLASTIC

FIRST HOMEV
ALPHABET

60+ Age-Perfect Reproducibles That Help Youngsters Learn Their Letters From A to Z

by Alyse Sweeney

NEW YORK • TORONTO • LONDON • AUCKLAND • SYDNEY
MEXICO CITY • NEW DELHI • HONG KONG • BUENOS AIRES

Teaching *Resources*

Edited by Elizabeth Bennett
Cover design by Brian LaRossa
Cover Illustraion by Peggy Tagel
Interior design by Brian LaRossa

ISBN-13: 978-0-545-15042-2
ISBN-10: 0-545-15042-6

5 6 7 8 9 10   40   15 14 13 12 11

TABLE OF CONTENTS

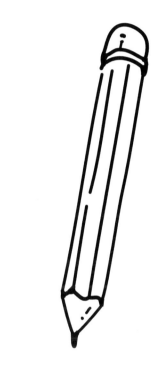

First Homework: Alphabet is filled with fun reproducible send-home pages that reinforce students' classroom learning.

Over the past decade, research has suggested that homework helps children develop skills and build study habits. Homework also fosters independence and responsibility—just what little ones crave! The letter to parents on page 5 includes a rationale for homework and tips for creating a positive homework environment.

First Homework is designed with a predictable format to encourage student independence and feelings of success. Each letter of the alphabet is paired with an engaging character whose name begins with that letter. An alligator, for example, guides students to recognize and write capital and lowercase a and to learn the sound a. Review pages throughout the book further support learning.

First Homework: Alphabet will help both teachers and parents accompany children down the thrilling road of learning and mastery.

Have a delightful journey!

—The Editors

FIRST HOMEWORK: ALPHABET meets these important standards.

- Visual letter recognition
- Sound-to-symbol correspondence
- Phonological awareness
- Letter formation

Mid-continent Research for Education and Learning is an organization that collects and synthesizes national and state K–12 curriculum standards.

Dear Parents,

This year, your child will bring home reproducible homework pages from Scholastic's **First Homework: Alphabet** book. These homework pages reinforce our classroom learning of letter recognition, letter formation, and letter sounds. Homework provides children with practice while fostering independence and responsibility—just what little ones crave!

As your child is new to homework, I'd like to share four ways to create a positive homework environment, from the Office of Educational Research and Improvement.

1. Show that you think homework is important. Provide a consistent time and place for it and turn off the television.

2. Offer help when needed, but let your child do as much as he or she can independently.

3. Check your child's work.

4. Talk to me if your child struggles with homework.

Homework is a great way to bring home and school closer together. Have fun watching your child grow and learn with these **First Homework** pages.

Sincerely,

_____

Name _____

Trace the **A** and **a** with your finger. Say **a**lligator.

Trace and write.

 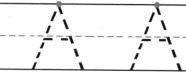

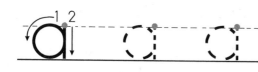

Circle each alligator with an **A** or **a**.

 A

a

 C

A

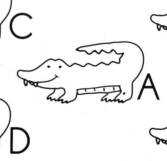 P

b

D

 a

Name _____

Draw a line from the alligator to each picture whose name begins with the letter a.

Name each picture. Listen to the first sound. Write the beginning letter for each picture.

B

Name

Bb

Trace the **B** and **b** with your finger. Say **b**at.

Trace and write.

B B B

b b b

Circle each bat with a B or b.

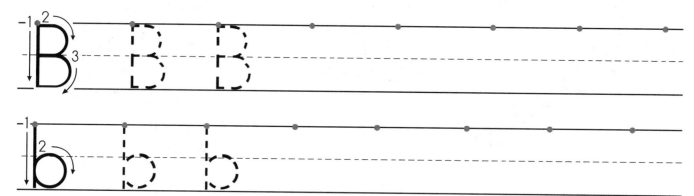

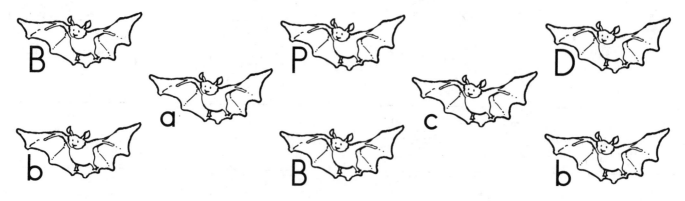

B   a

P   c   D

b   B   b

Name _____

Bb

Draw a line from the bat to each picture whose name begins with the letter b.

Name each picture. Listen to the first sound. Write the beginning letter for each picture.

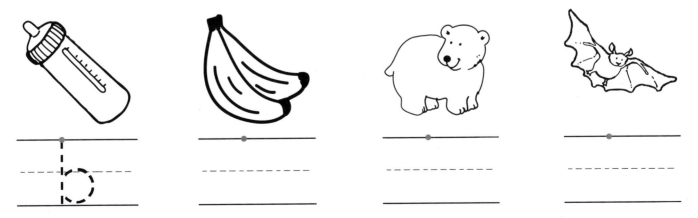

Name _____

Trace and write.

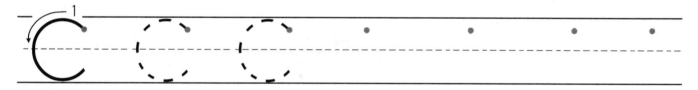

Circle each cat with a C or c.

Name _____

Draw a line from the cat to each picture whose name begins with the letter c.

Name each picture. Listen to the first sound. Write the beginning letter for each picture.

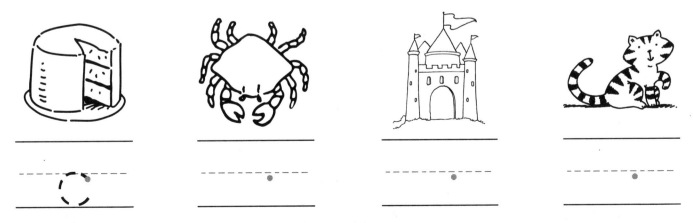

D

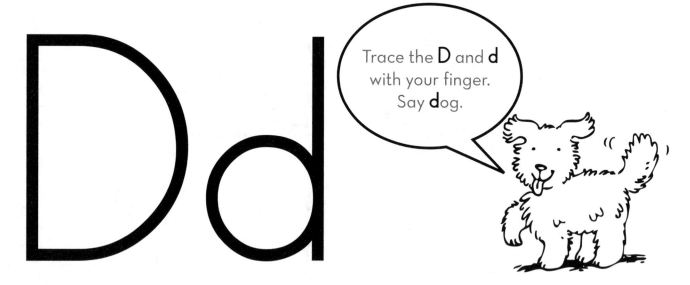

Trace the D and d with your finger. Say dog.

Trace and write.

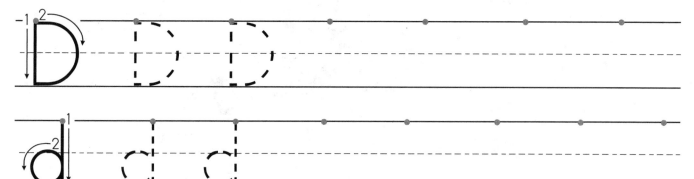

Circle each dog with a D or d.

d

P

T

a

C

D

D

d

D

Name _____

Dd

Draw a line from the dog to each picture whose name begins with the letter d.

Name each picture. Listen to the first sound. Write the beginning letter for each picture.

E

Name _____

E e

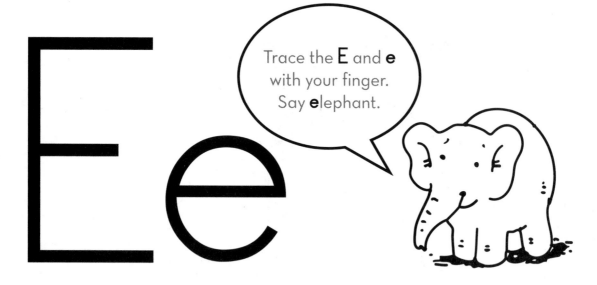

Trace the **E** and **e** with your finger. Say **e**lephant.

Trace and write.

E

e

Circle each elephant with an E or e.

 e

 a

 E

 F

 e

 E

 g

 C

14   First Homework: Alphabet • Scholastic Teaching Resources

Name _____

E e

Draw a line from the elephant to each picture whose name begins with the letter e.

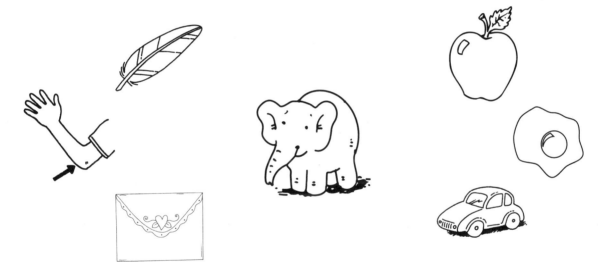

Name each picture. Listen to the first sound. Write the beginning letter for each picture.

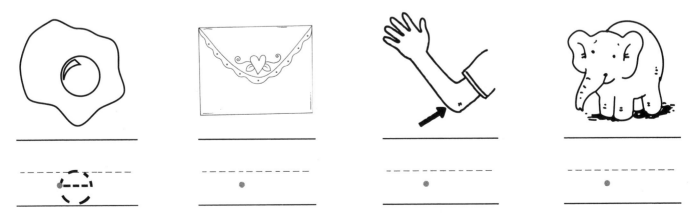

Name _____

Trace each letter. Then write the letter in the space.

Name _____

Draw a line from each lowercase letter to the matching uppercase letter.

a

b

c

d

e

B

E

D

C

A

Name _____

Draw a line from each letter to the picture whose name begins with that letter.

B

C

E

A

D

Name _____

Name each picture. Listen to the first sound. Then circle the beginning letter for each picture.

c a b

d c b

e b c

a b e

F

Name _____

Trace the **F** and **f** with your finger. Say **f**ish.

Trace and write.

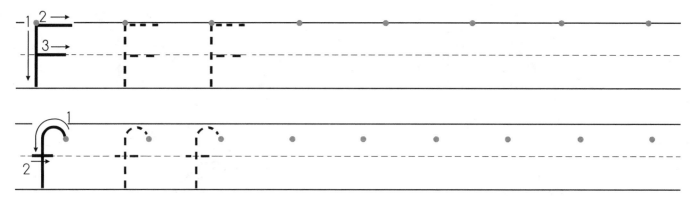

Circle each fish with an F or f.

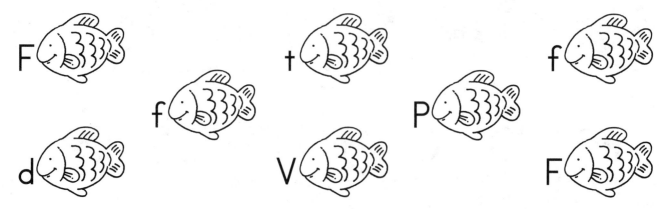

F   f   d   t   V   P   f   F

Name _____

Ff

Draw a line from the fish to each picture whose name begins with the letter f.

Name each picture. Listen to the first sound. Write the beginning letter for each picture.

Name

Trace the **G** and **g** with your finger. Say **g**oat.

Trace and write.

 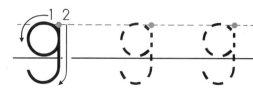

Circle each goat with a **G** or **g**.

p    g   C   f   G

G    z   g

Name _____

Gg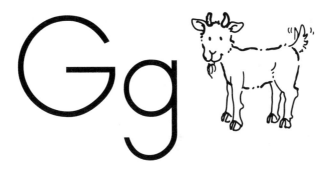

Draw a line from the goat to each picture whose name begins with the letter g.

Name each picture. Listen to the first sound. Write the beginning letter for each picture.

Name _____

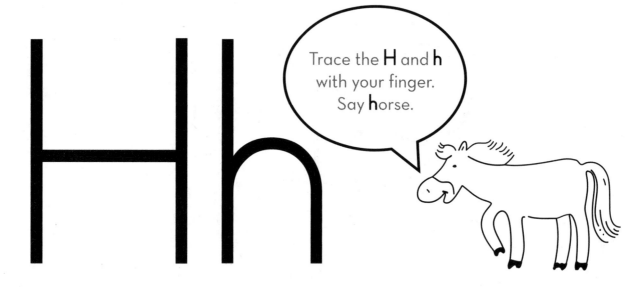

Trace the **H** and **h** with your finger. Say **h**orse.

Trace and write.

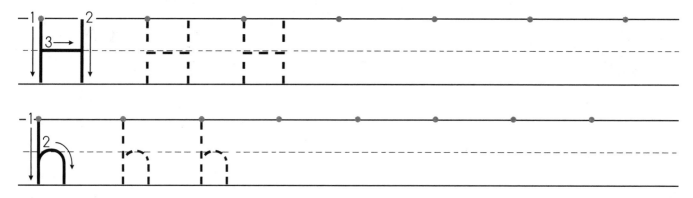

Circle each horse with an H or h.

Name _____

Draw a line from the horse to each picture whose name begins with the letter h.

Name each picture. Listen to the first sound. Write the beginning letter for each picture.

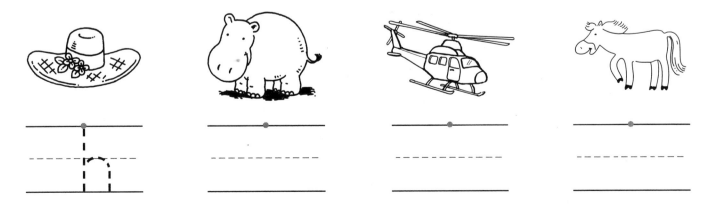

Name _____

I i

Trace the I and i with your finger. Say iguana.

Trace and write.

Circle each iguana with an I or i.

Name _____

Draw a line from the iguana to each picture whose name begins with the letter i.

Name each picture. Listen to the first sound. Write the beginning letter for each picture.

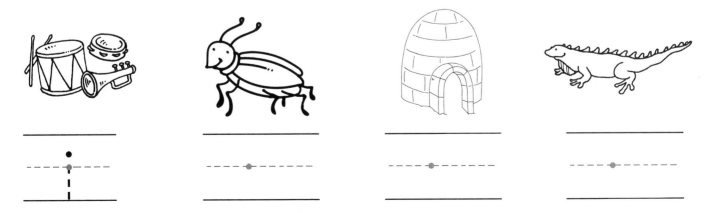

J

Name _____

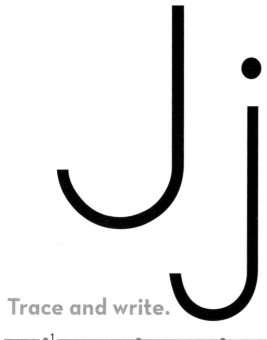

Trace the J and j with your finger. Say jellyfish.

Trace and write.

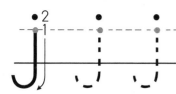

Circle each jellyfish with a J or j.

 j

 r

 i

 J

 p

 T

 j

 J

Name _____

J j

Draw a line from the jellyfish to each picture whose name begins with the letter j.

Name each picture. Listen to the first sound. Write the beginning letter for each picture.

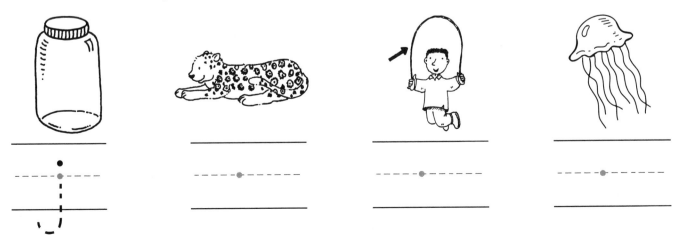

Name _____

Trace each letter. Then write the letter in the space.

Name _____

Draw a line from each lowercase letter to the matching uppercase letter.

f   H

g   G

h   F

i   J

j   I

Name _____

Draw a line from each letter to the picture whose name begins with that letter.

G

H

J

F

I

Name _____

Name each picture. Listen to the first sound. Then circle the beginning letter for each picture.

i   g   j   h   f   g

h   j   i   g   f   h

Name _____

K k

Trace the **K** and **k** with your finger. Say **k**angaroo.

Trace and write.

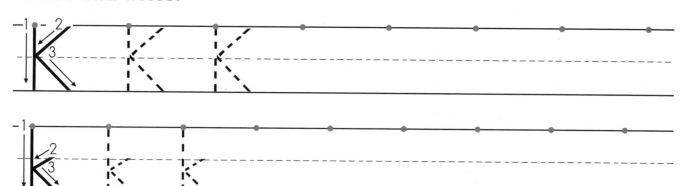

Circle each kangaroo with a K or k.

f
k

K

K
p

b

P
k

Name

Draw a line from the kangaroo to each picture whose name begins with the letter k.

Name each picture. Listen to the first sound. Write the beginning letter for each picture.

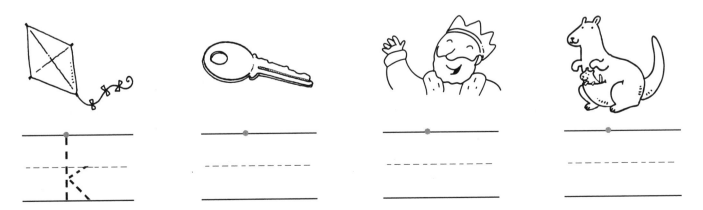

L

Name _____

L l

Trace the L and l with your finger. Say lion.

Trace and write.

Circle each lion with an L or l.

 L

 t

 L F

 b

 T l

L l

Name _____

L

L l

Draw a line from the lion to each picture whose name begins with the letter l.

Name each picture. Listen to the first sound. Write the beginning letter for each picture.

Name

Trace the **M** and **m** with your finger. Say **m**ouse.

Trace and write.

Circle each mouse with an **M** or **m**.

 m

 e

 D

 m

 M

 M

 E

 N

Name _____

Mm

Draw a line from the mouse to each picture whose name begins with the letter m.

Name each picture. Listen to the first sound. Write the beginning letter for each picture.

N

Name _____

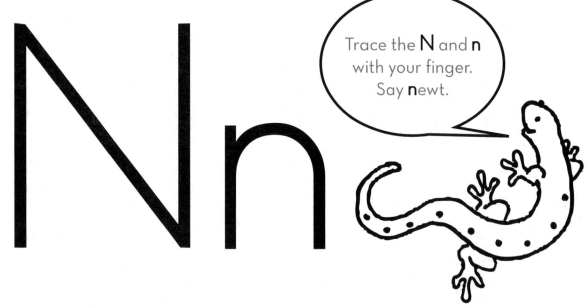

Trace the **N** and **n** with your finger. Say **n**ewt.

Trace and write.

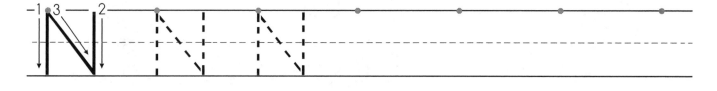

Circle each newt with an **N** or **n**.

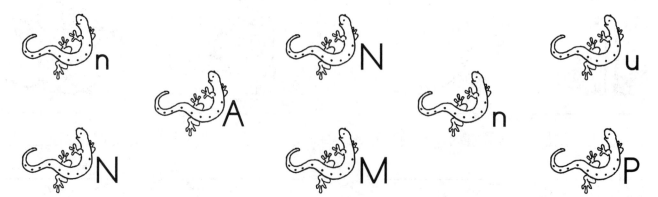

Nn

Draw a line from the newt to each picture whose name begins with the letter n.

Name each picture. Listen to the first sound. Write the beginning letter for each picture.

Name

Trace the **O** and **o** with your finger. Say **o**strich.

Trace and write.

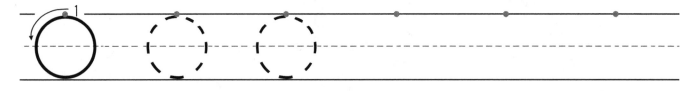

Circle each ostrich with an O or o.

o

O

C

o

O

a

E

A

Name _____

Draw a line from the ostrich to each picture whose name begins with the letter o.

Name each picture. Listen to the first sound. Write the beginning letter for each picture.

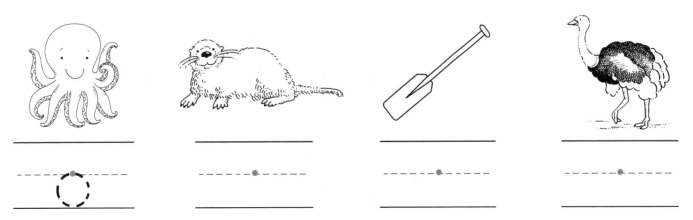

Name _____

Trace each letter. Then write the letter in the space.

Name _____

Draw a line from each lowercase letter to the matching uppercase letter.

k

l

m

n

o

L

K

O

N

M

Name _____

Draw a line from each letter to the picture whose name begins with that letter.

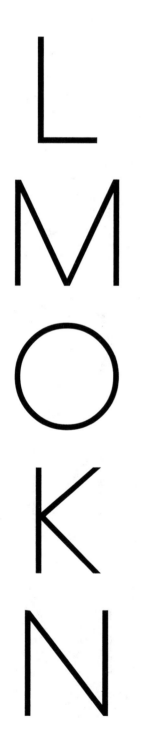

Name _____

Name each picture. Listen to the first sound. Then circle the beginning letter for each picture.

m   n   k

n   l   o

l   k   n

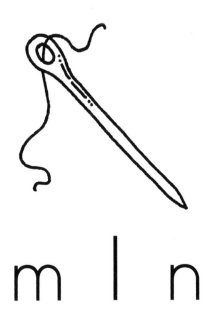

m   l   n

Name _____

P p

Trace the **P** and **p** with your finger. Say **p**ig.

Trace and write.

Circle each pig with a P or p.

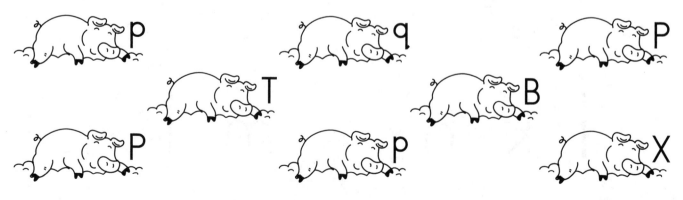

Name _____

P p

Draw a line from the pig to each picture whose name begins with the letter p.

Name each picture. Listen to the first sound. Write the beginning letter for each picture.

Name

Q q

Trace the **Q** and **q** with your finger. Say **q**ueen.

Trace and write.

Circle each queen with a Q or q.

Name _____

Qq

Draw a line from the queen to each picture whose name begins with the letter q.

Name each picture. Listen to the first sound. Write the beginning letter for each picture.

q _____   _____   _____   _____

R

Name _____

R r

Trace the **R** and **r** with your finger. Say **r**accoon.

Trace and write.

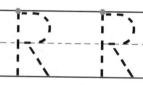
R R R

r r r

Circle each raccoon with an **R** or **r**.

 R    P    r

 t    R

 r    e    D

Name _____

Rr

Draw a line from the raccoon to each picture whose name begins with the letter r.

Name each picture. Listen to the first sound. Write the beginning letter for each picture.

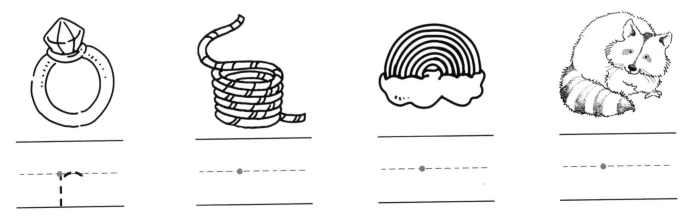

r _____   _____   _____   _____

Name _____

S s

Trace the S and s
with your finger.
Say seal.

Trace and write.

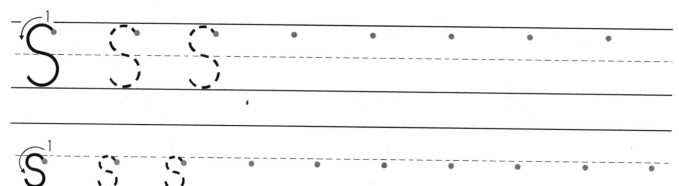

S S S · · · · · ·

s s s · · · · · · ·

Circle each seal with an S or s.

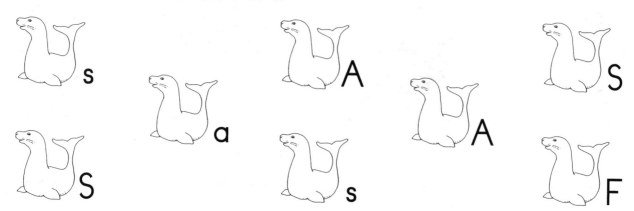

s

a

S

A

A

s

S

F

Name _____

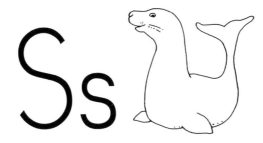

Ss

Draw a line from the seal to each picture whose name begins with the letter s.

Name each picture. Listen to the first sound. Write the beginning letter for each picture.

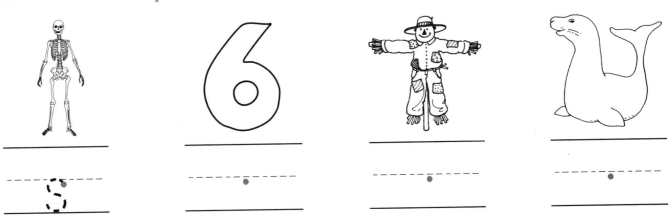

S ____

T

Name _____

T t

Trace the T and t with your finger. Say turtle.

Trace and write.

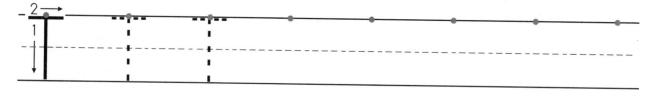

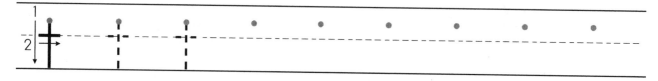

Circle each turtle with a T or t.

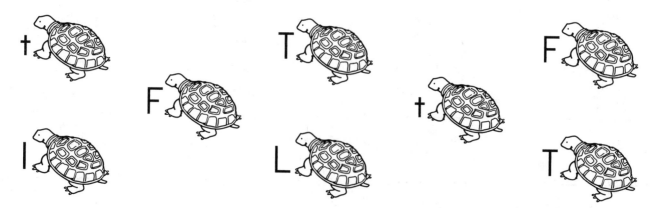

Name _____

Draw a line from the turtle to each picture whose name begins with the letter t.

Name each picture. Listen to the first sound. Write the beginning letter for each picture.

Name

Trace each letter. Then write the letter in the space.

P

Q

R

S

T

Name

Draw a line from each lowercase letter to the matching uppercase letter.

p

q

r

s

t

T

S

R

Q

P

Name _____

Draw a line from each letter to the picture whose name begins with that letter.

Name _____

Name each picture. Listen to the first sound. Then circle the beginning letter for each picture.

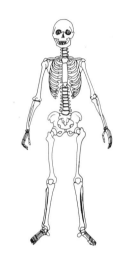

q t s

t r s

r p t

r s p

U

Name _____

U u

Trace the **U** and **u** with your finger. Say **u**mbrella.

Trace and write.

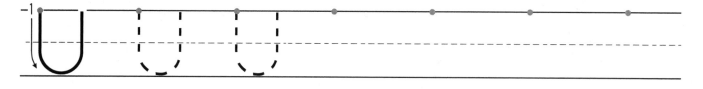

Circle each umbrella with a U or u.

 a

 U

 u

 v

 e

 o

 U

 u

Name _____

Uu

Draw a line from the umbrella to each picture whose name begins with the letter u.

Name each picture. Listen to the first sound. Write the beginning letter for each picture.

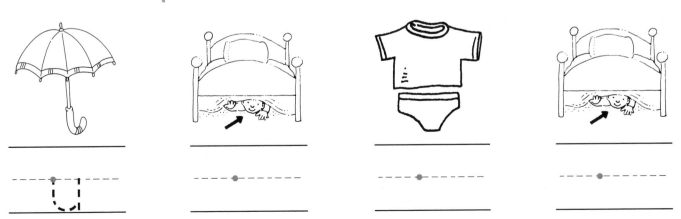

Name _____

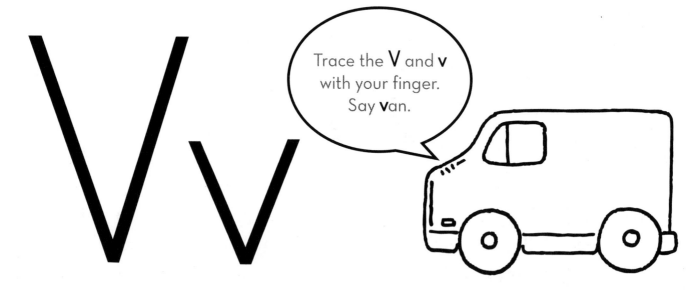

Trace the V and v with your finger. Say van.

Trace and write.

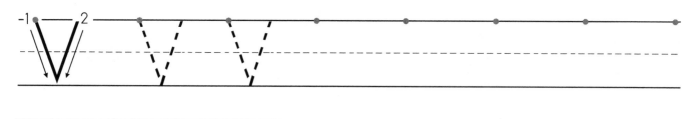

Circle each van with a V or v.

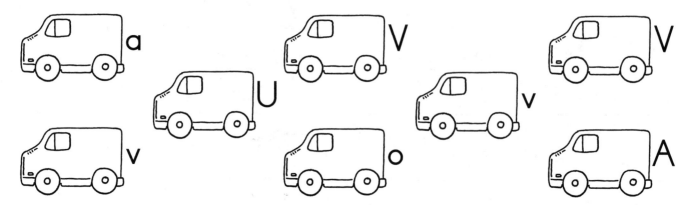

Name _____

Vv

Draw a line from the van to each picture whose name begins with the letter v.

Name each picture. Listen to the first sound. Write the beginning letter for each picture.

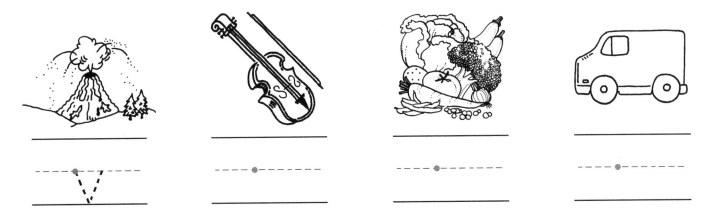

W

Name _____

Trace the **W** and **w** with your finger. Say **w**alrus.

Trace and write.

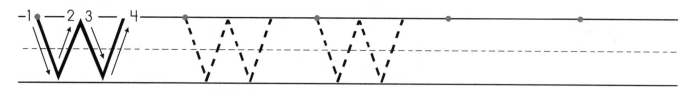

Circle each walrus with a **W** or **w**.

R

w

W

m

r

W

M

w

Name _____

Ww

Draw a line from the walrus to each picture whose name begins with the letter w.

Name each picture. Listen to the first sound. Write the beginning letter for each picture.

Name _____

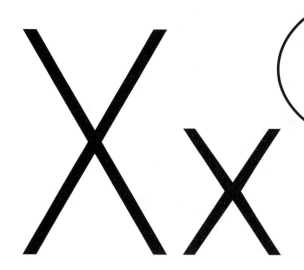 

Trace the **X** and **x** with your finger. Say **X**-ray.

Trace and write.

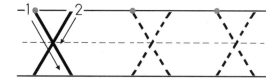

Circle each X-ray with an X or x.

 v

 X

 W

 x

 X

 x

 W

 z

Name _____

Draw a line from the X-ray to each picture whose name begins with the letter x.

Name each picture. Listen to the first sound. Write the beginning letter for each picture.

Name

Y y

Trace the **Y** and **y** with your finger. Say **y**ak.

Trace and write.

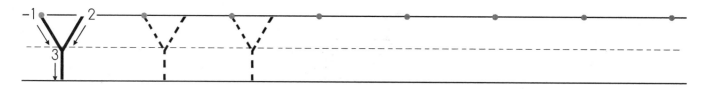

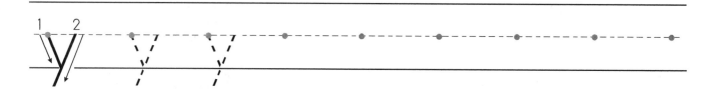

Circle each yak with a Y or y.

Name _____

Yy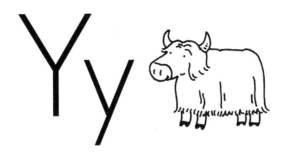

Draw a line from the yak to each picture whose name begins with the letter y.

Name each picture. Listen to the first sound. Write the beginning letter for each picture.

Name _____

Z z

Trace the **Z** and **z** with your finger. Say **z**ebra.

Trace and write.

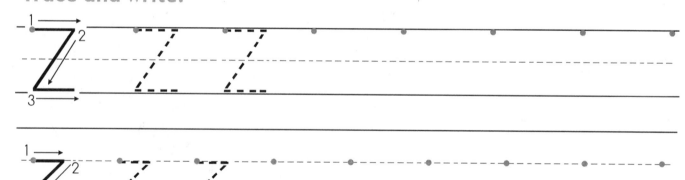

Circle each zebra with a **Z** or **z**.

 Z

 z

 s

 x

 Z

 y

 V

 z

Name _____

Zz

Draw a line from the zebra to each picture whose name begins with the letter z.

Name each picture. Listen to the first sound. Write the beginning letter for each picture.

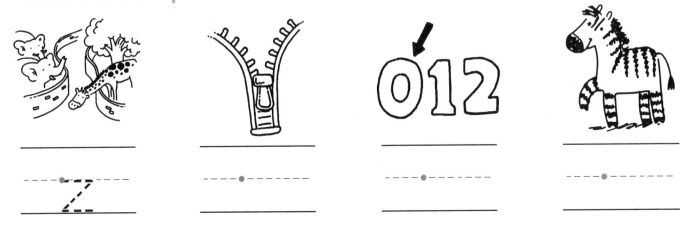

z _____ _____ _____ _____

Name _____

Trace each letter. Then write the letter in the space.

Name

Draw a line from each lowercase letter to the matching uppercase letter.

u

v

w

x

y

z

Y

Z

V

W

X

U

Name _____

Draw a line from each letter to the picture whose name begins with that letter.

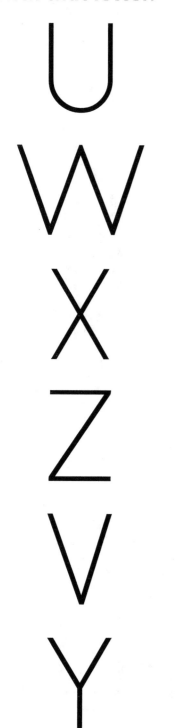

Name

Name each picture. Listen to the first sound. Then circle the beginning letter for each picture.

X   V   W

y   X   W

Z   W   X

V   W   Z

ANSWER KEY

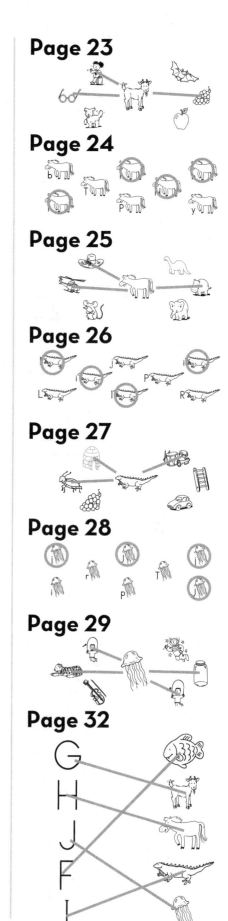

Page 33

Page 34

Page 35

Page 36

Page 37

Page 38

Page 39

Page 40

Page 41

Page 42

Page 43

Page 46

Page 47

Page 48

Page 49

Page 50

Page 51

Page 52

Page 53

Page 54

Page 55

Page 56

ANSWER KEY

Page 57

Page 60

Page 61

Page 62

Page 63

Page 64

Page 65

Page 66

Page 67

Page 68

Page 69

Page 70

Page 71

Page 72

Page 73

Page 76

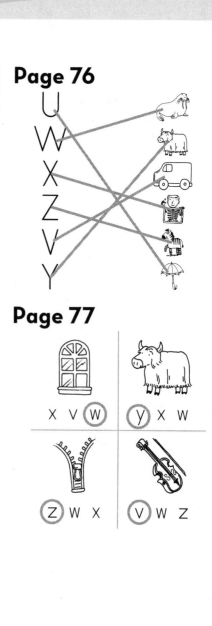

Page 77